TABLE OF CONTENTS

Introduction

What do you do when you stop believing in a cause you've championed for almost a decade? That's where I found myself when I wrote the first edition of this book in 2016.

Since starting my own marketing consulting business in 2007, I've been a woman on a mission. To anyone willing to listen - and many who were not - I would assert my view on the need for a laser-sharp target market, a clear marketing message, and a detailed strategy for delivering the message in a way that makes money. Nothing wrong with that, except that it seldom works. There's a reason why more than 90% of start-ups fail and it's certainly not because they messed up their marketing.

First, a disclaimer: The content of the book isn't for everyone. If you're happy with where you are in your business, this probably isn't for you. If you're in business simply to make money, this book **definitely** isn't for you. Being in business to make money is like saying you want fruit salad to eat fruit. It's a given. Fruit salad isn't filled with vegetables.

In the same way, a business that isn't run with the primary purpose of making money isn't a business so for now, let's just agree that we're all in business to make money otherwise we would be a charity. The focus of this book is on the OTHER reasons we're in business.

Another reason why running a business focused only on making money is a bad idea: The chase for money is usually rooted in the lack of it and that's bad news for the *Law of Attraction!*

According to the *Law of Attraction*, like attracts like and if you're running your business from a mindset of lack, it's a certainty that you'll attract customers with exactly the same mindset. Or no customers at all!

Do you really want leads that don't turn into customers, or customers who are price conscious? Or would you rather want to attract potential customers willing to pay you what you're truly worth with all the optional extras?

When you take money out of the equation, why are you in business? You should be able to come up with a list of reasons why you've taken the plunge into entrepreneurship, ultimately because you wanted to live the life of your dreams free of financial restrictions.

So is this book for you? If you want to know how to build a successful business in order to live the life of your dreams, then no. But if you want to know how to live the life of your dreams while building a successful business, I think you'll enjoy the read. All I ask is that you keep an open mind. At the very least, you might get a glimpse into a life of endless possibilities.

Please note: The content of this book is heavily influenced by the teachings of Abraham as delivered by Esther and Jerry Hicks.

About me

The decision to start a business is a big one. It's the moment you decide to take your future into your own hands and build the life you could never have while you're working for a boss.

I remember that exact day.

On Valentine's Day, 2007, I gave myself the biggest gift of love by resigning from a job with a stable, full-time salary to pursue my life-long dream of having my own business. I thought I had it waxed! With a post-graduate qualification in my pocket, years of business experience behind me, and positivity that could last a lifetime, I was ready to take on the world.

So imagine my annoyance at a colleague's parting words: *"Best wishes on your journey. There will be hard times, but just keep on believing."*

What was he talking about? Hard times? I knew exactly what I was doing. With the growing opportunities of the Internet, being an entrepreneur was easier than ever.

Not so! My fall was hard.

The truth is that no amount of study, experience, hard work or positivity could've prepared me for the difficult road that is entrepreneurship. It doesn't matter what you think you know, your true learning as an entrepreneur begins only once you're in it. The irony is that I'm a marketer and my specialist area is marketing strategy! Yet those were the areas in my business with which I struggled most.

What I was taught to be true in Marketing 101 and practiced religiously in business since the early 90s was suddenly being challenged by the rise of the Internet. There were new rules. But did the new rules replace the old rules or did they change the old rules? Was marketing evolving into an entirely new discipline? Was what I knew about marketing now null and void?

Not only were my thoughts on business and marketing challenged, entrepreneurship also challenged my values, priorities, relationships, health, finances, and life. I can't remember the number of times I had to start over again, not just picking up the pieces of my business, but picking up the pieces of who I was as a person.

This is where I giggle. When I wrote the first version of this book in 2016, this is where I said *"It took me more than a decade to be able to say I made it through to the other side as one whole person."* Just when you think you have it all figured out, the Universe responds with *'Hold my beer!'* and sends more challenges for you to grow even more, so it's been an interesting five years since then...especially with COVID-19 in the mix.

Nevertheless, I wouldn't change my journey for the world! What I'm most grateful for is that the core business fundamentals that seemed to fall apart were the same fundamentals I could rely on to put the pieces back together. Now with old and new knowledge combined, I'm able to see the big picture of business as it is today. Most importantly, I have learnt to see my business in the big picture of my life. It is this big picture that I aim to share with you in this guide.

If you're new to entrepreneurship, I'd like to say to you: *"Best wishes on your journey. There will be hard times, but just keep on believing."* I hope that through this guide, I'll make the road less bumpy and much more fun. Because, above all else, entrepreneurship should be fun.

PART 1: It's not business, it's spiritual

Chapter 1 - Challenge your old thinking patterns

Where do I begin?

Despite being an entrepreneur for most of my life, all my hard work was yielding less and less rewards at greater costs to me and to my family with constant stress and pressure of not knowing enough, having enough, or doing enough.

Whether you've just started out or whether you've been in business for a while, there's no doubt you'll face your fair share of challenges. Especially now! Millions of entrepreneurs across the globe are trying to survive the 2020 plague (otherwise known as COVID-19).

Depending on where you are, these challenges can seem huge, but I've learnt that the problems we face as entrepreneurs come down to only three variables: time, money, and knowledge.

On a scale of 1 to 10, where do you find yourself in terms of availability of time and money? Take a look at Figure 1.

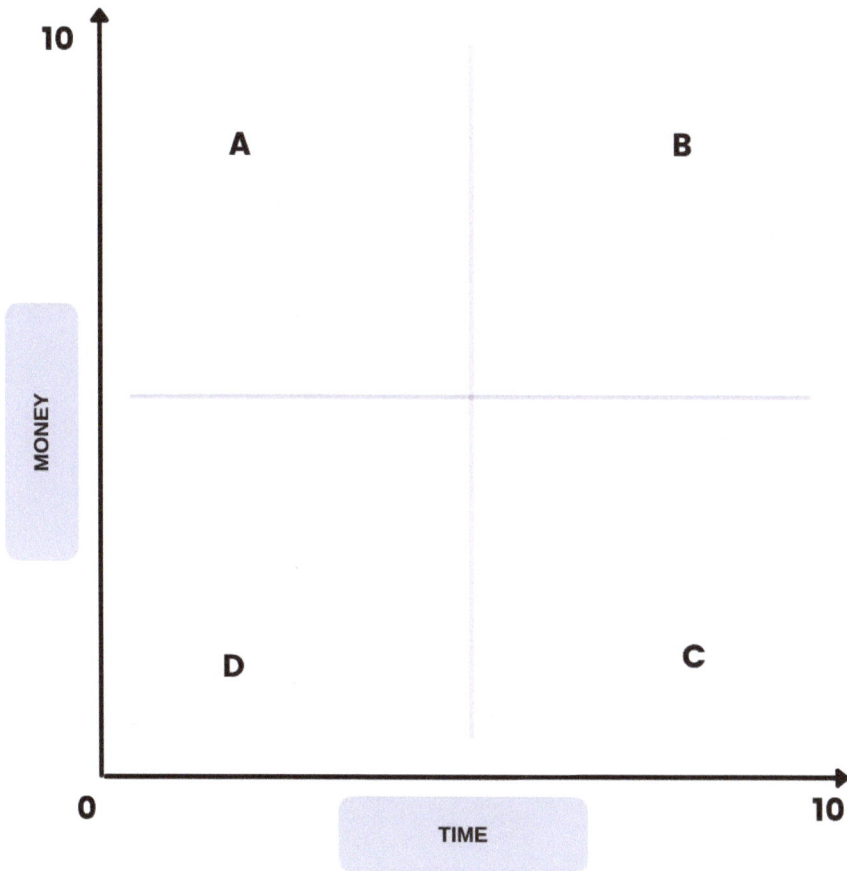

Figure 1: The 4 Quadrants of Lack

As an entrepreneur, you're always striving to get to Quadrant B where you can have enough time and money to invest in your business:

- A, sufficient money to invest in your business but limited time.
- **B, sufficient time and sufficient money to invest in your business.**
- C, sufficient time and limited money and to invest in your business.
- D, limited time and limited money to invest.

How do you get to B? Often you choose the route of doing more, learning more, or taking on additional money-making opportunities on your path to achieving financial abundance.

Which raises the ultimate question: How do you KNOW exactly what needs to happen to finally achieve financial abundance? How do you decide where to invest your limited time and money? Just when you think you know it all, life throws in new uncertainties.

Nothing like complicating matters even further. You'll now find yourself in one of 8 triangles, each causing its own frustration.

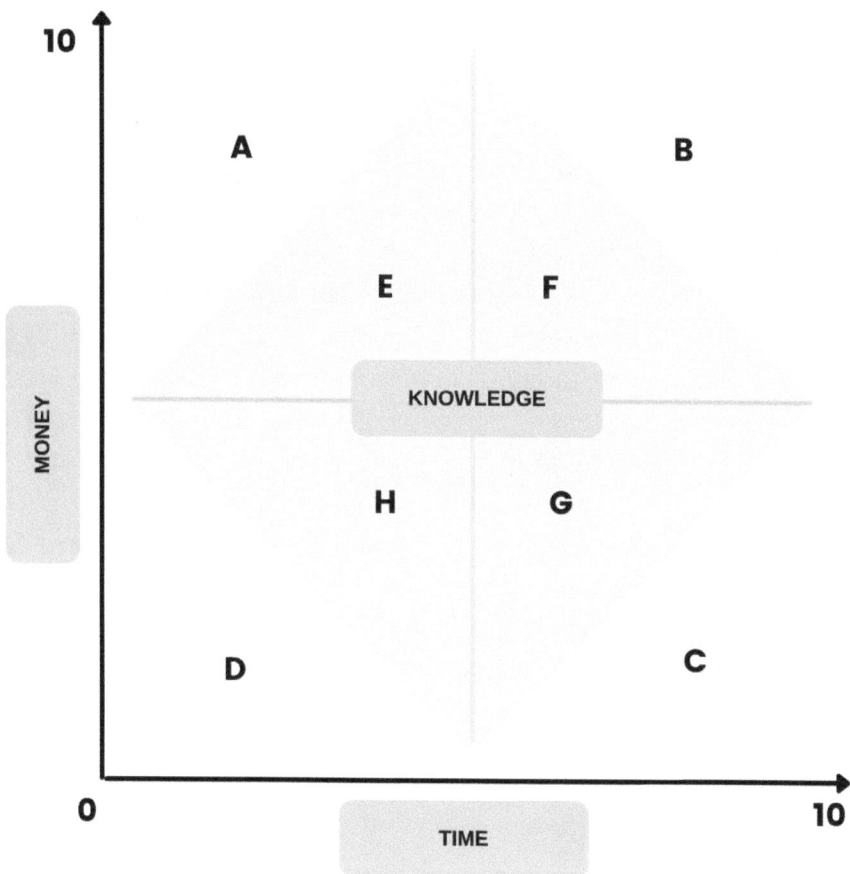

Figure 2 - The 8 Frustrations

Triangles A, B, C, and D deals with **lack of knowledge**:

- **A.** I don't know enough about business and I have limited time to do everything myself anyway. Fortunately, I have money to pay someone to help me get it done right.
  Frustration: From all there is to do around business, how do I know who the right people are to help me run a successful business?

- **B.** I don't know enough about business. Fortunately, I have enough time to learn what I need to learn, take on the tasks that I enjoy doing, and then pay someone to help me do the rest successfully.
  Frustration: From all there is to know about business, how do I know what I need to learn and who the right people are to help me run a successful business?

- **C.** I don't know enough about business and I don't have enough money to take all the premium business courses. Fortunately, I have sufficient time to invest in learning what I need to learn.
  Frustration: From all there is to know about business, how do I know what I need to learn?

- **D.** I don't know enough about business, I have limited time to learn everything I need to learn, and limited money to pay people to help me run a successful business.
  Frustration: From all there is to know about business and everything that needs to be done, how do I maximise my limited resources?

Triangles E, F, G, and H deals with **sufficient knowledge**:

- **E.** I know enough about business, but there's not enough time to implement everything myself. Fortunately, I have enough money to pay people to help me run a successful business.
  Frustration: From all there is to do around business, how do I know who the right people are to help me run a successful business?

- **F.** I know enough about business. I also have enough time to learn more, take on the tasks that I enjoy doing, and then pay people to help me run a successful business.
  Frustration: From all there is to know about business, how do I know what I need to learn and who the right people are to help

me run a successful business?

- **G.** I know enough about business. While I may not have enough money to pay people to help me run a successful business, I have enough time to keep on top of business trends and advance my skills.
  Frustration: How do I know what I need to learn to build a sustainable business?

- **H.** I know enough about business. Unfortunately, I have limited time to keep up with business trends and limited money to pay people to help me run a successful business.
  Frustration: How do I identify the right courses to take, people to follow, and webinars to attend given my limited time and money?

Entrepreneurship is a constant juggle between all triangles!

Are you currently in the first section and you're struggling with a lack of knowledge as well as lacking time or money? Or are in section two when you know what you need to know, but you don't have the money or time to do it?

Irrespective of which triangle you find yourself in, entrepreneurship is an on-going search for knowledge and personal growth and herein lies the challenge: What determines how you progress from where you are to where you want to be depends on how you handle any lack of knowledge. It becomes a balancing act of knowing how to maximise your own inherent strengths, learning what you need to learn, and realising when to hand over the rest to the right people with the right skills.

Sadly, the life of the entrepreneur becomes an endless loop of trial and error with the end result often being an overwhelming feeling of failure as we try to figure this out. We get bogged down by our mistakes of the past and begin to act from a place of desperation, not inspiration. And when we're running a business rooted in desperation and lack, we lose our ability to dream. We completely forget why we started our business in the first place.

Sound familiar? The great news is that you can change your life simply by changing the way you think!

Consider some of my favourite quotes from my favourite people.

> *"Life is really very simple. What we give out we get back. Every thought we think is creating our future."* Louise Hay

> *"What the mind of a man can conceive and believe, it can achieve."* Napoleon Hill

> *"You are the Michelangelo of your own life. The David that you are sculpting is you. And you do it with your thoughts."* Joe Vitale

> *"Happiness does not depend on who you are or what you have. It solely relies on what you think."* Buddha

What they're referring to is the *Law of Attraction*: What we think determines how we feel. How we feel determines our level of vibration. Our level of vibration determines the people and situations we attract.

It's a law and it works for everyone whether we believe in it or not; whether we like it or not. Your circumstances as they are today, like them or not, are all your own doing. Tough to accept, isn't it? It isn't the lack of money, or lack of time, or lack of knowledge. While those issues may very well be present, they're not the reasons why your business isn't flourishing.

A common way to demonstrate the *Law of Attraction* is through the example of the tuning fork first used by Dr. Masaru Emoto, author of the New York Times best-seller, *The Hidden Messages of Water*. Emoto works with three tuning forks. Forks 1 and 2 are designed to vibrate 440 times per second, while Fork 3 vibrates 442 times per second. When he hits Fork 1 with a rubber hammer, Fork 2 immediately vibrates and gives off a sound because it resonates with Fork.

However, Fork 3 remains silent. This shows that energies vibrating at the same frequencies somehow find each other.

Now this is where you decide whether or not the contents of this book are for you. Are you willing to entertain the idea that, when creating a thriving business, managing your vibration from one moment to the next is as important as managing your time, money, and knowledge?

If you're still not convinced, it's time to bring in the science.

According to quantum physics, everything is energy and it vibrates at its own frequency, even emotions.

Figure 3 depicts the frequencies of emotions as a hierarchy of human consciousness where positive emotions, such as joy, love, peace, knowledge, empowerment, enlightenment, and freedom are right at the top. Negative emotions, including fear, grief, shame, and unworthiness are towards the bottom. In between, you'll find everything else.

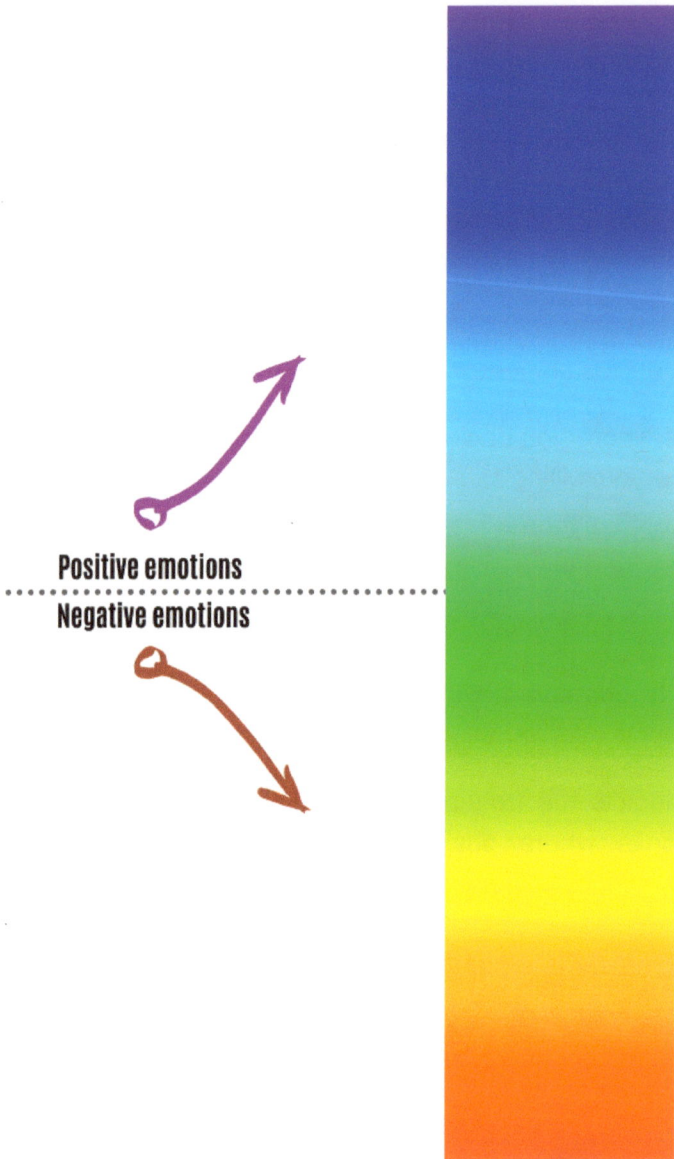

Figure 3 - Tuning your vibration

Give it a try. Think of situations that evoke different emotions. What does anger feel like to you? Guilt? Shame? Love?

When we linger too long in the shame, guilt, apathy, unworthiness, and fear of having too little time, money, or knowledge, we attract people, situations, and things that perpetuate our suffering and the feeling of just getting by. When we let go of the fear and the negative energy and start seeing everything from a perspective of unconditional love, we begin to build a business led by spirit energy as we tap into unlimited consciousness and its universal wisdom.

Are you still with me?

You could either discard this as "airy-fairy" and impractical and continue doing what you've been doing...with the likelihood of achieving the same results. Or you could suspend all judgement and entertain the idea that the first step to building a successful business starts with fine-tuning your vibration.

When you put in the time and effort to work on your **emotions,** you're able to automatically and effortlessly attract the life of your dreams no matter what challenges you may face. As you tap into your divine knowledge from a space of love, empowerment, and peace, insights will appear out of nowhere, and everything will unfold exactly as it should in due time. Abundance will flow to you as you need it because, believe in it or not, the *Law of Attraction* never fails.

When you introduce the *Law of Attraction* into the equation, building a successful business even looks like more fun! As illustrated in Figure 4, when you're filled with positive emotions, such as gratitude, appreciation, love, peace, and joy, **knowledge** comes to you in the form of inspiration, intuition, and chance encounters with the right people. Money and time becomes secondary as you have everything you need in that moment.

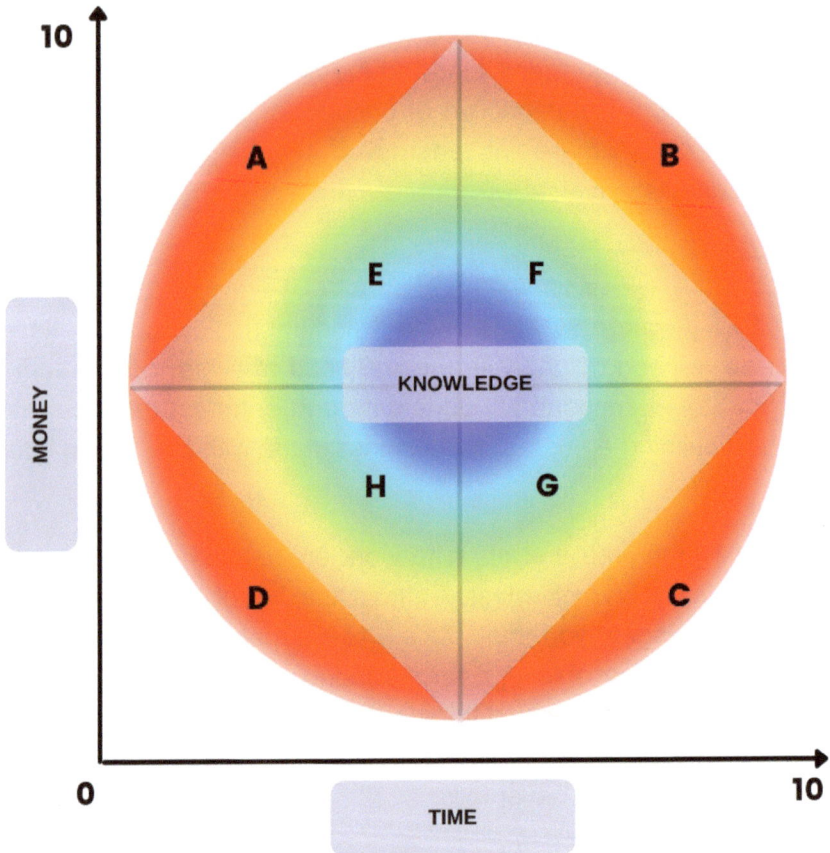

Figure 4 - Tuning your vibration as an antidote to lack

So are you willing to change your old thinking patterns and embrace the principles of the *Law of Attraction*? The following chapters describe the steps I used to implement the *Law of Attraction* in my life and transform my thinking and, in so doing, my business.

My wish is that it will do the same for you.

Chapter 2 - Tell the story of your life the way you want it to be

As a Marketing Consultant, I love working with start-up businesses because their enthusiasm, passion and ability to dream big is contagious. But the soul-destroying part of my job is that I seldom get to see them move beyond the starting blocks. Each time their fire dies, a little part of me dies with them.

Of course, that only highlighted my own issues as a Marketing Consultant. I began to doubt everything that I was doing because, despite my best efforts, their ventures were failing. The irony is that I'm an ardent student of the *Law of Attraction*. In fact, if a $10 online certification has any clout, I'm a *Certified Law of Attraction Basic Practitioner!*

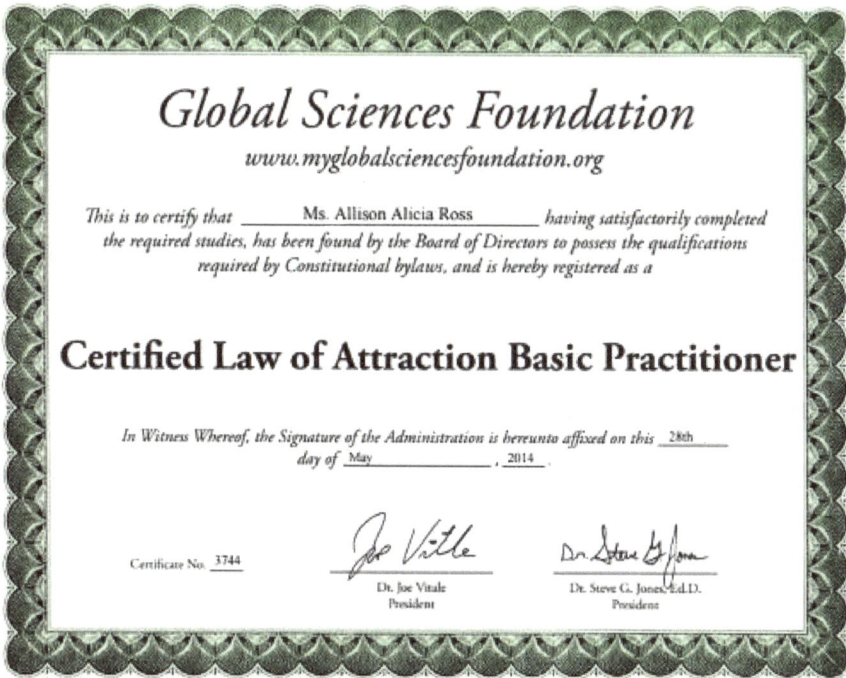

Figure 5 - Law of Attraction Certificate

I knew this stuff, yet I was unable to see the glaringly obvious flaw in my own thinking that was attracting the wrong clients to my business.

I was telling a very negative story about my business and its effect on my life that went something like this: *"I don't enjoy working with start-ups because few move beyond starting up. They don't have money to pay for my services so I spend most of my time working for free, which is stopping me from moving forward in my own life. Maybe I shouldn't be a Marketing Consultant"*.

And yet I continued to spend money on marketing tools, courses, and advertising to attract those very same types of clients. Insane, isn't it?

I don't know exactly when or how it happened, but suddenly in one moment of one day, the insanity of it all just hit me. It was in that moment when I made the decision to stop being someone who's trying to manage time, money and my lack of knowledge with horrendous results. Instead I became someone who embraced the *Law of Attraction*.

That entailed stopping absolutely everything that I was doing! No more buying shiny new objects, no more learning, no more advertising. For a solid week it was just me doing the things I love doing, including watching hours and hours of reruns of my favourite TV shows; taking time away from my laptop to have fun with my family and friends; sleeping a minimum of eight hours a night; and reading inspirational books.

One of the greatest benefits of fully embracing the *Law of Attraction* is the clarity you gain from stepping out of the typical problem-solving mode in which entrepreneurs operate. The more time I spent raising my vibration by doing the things I enjoyed away from business, the clearer the vision and goals for my business became.

I'm usually not one to write down my visions and my goals. I admit, when it comes to self-discipline, I'm a work-in-progress. A trick I learnt recently that works really well for me is to write my goals in the form of a story. From a place of clarity, I was able to rewrite the story of my life the way I want it to be.

"*I love working with start-up businesses because their enthusiasm, passion and ability to dream big is contagious. My biggest reward is seeing my clients overcome their fears and grow into thriving businesses. I thoroughly enjoy the financial freedom of doing what I want whenever I want, and I'm particularly grateful that my unlimited income allows me to spend time doing what I love with the people I love.*"

How would you rewrite the story of your life?

Make your story as detailed as possible. The more the details, the greater the momentum. The greater the momentum, the greater the vibration.

CAUTION: Make sure you're telling a story that makes you feel good! You do not want to activate momentum in the wrong direction so use positive words, such as "*grateful*", "*thankful*", "*passionate*", and "*love*".

For example, I could add to my story that I love taking early-morning walks on the beach and that I'm thankful to be living in Cape Town, so close to the sea. I could add that I'm grateful for places with Wi-Fi connectivity that allow me to work from anywhere I choose. One of the things I'm incredibly grateful for is that being an entrepreneur allows me to decide how to spend my day, especially when that means taking an afternoon nap or spending the day at the mall. These all need to make my list because these are the little things that make me happy. Are you up for a challenge?

Exercise 1

Write the new story of your new clients and new life. Include all the activities you love and those you'd like to participate in if time and money were no longer an issue. Use positive affirmation such as "*love*" and "*appreciate*," and be as descriptive as possible using words that appeal to the five senses.

Here's my full new story, for example:

"I love working with start-up businesses because their enthusiasm, passion and ability to dream big is contagious. My biggest reward is seeing my clients overcome their fears and grow into thriving businesses. I thoroughly enjoy the financial freedom of doing what I want whenever I want, and I'm particularly grateful that my unlimited income allows me to spend time doing what I love with the people I love.

I love the early morning crispness of the beach and the feel of the cold, wet sand beneath my feet; I love the smell of the ocean, and when I see its vastness I appreciate that I'm part of a vibrant, thriving, powerful universe. I appreciate the freedom that working from a coffee shop brings me; the smell of fresh percolated coffee awakens my senses and the random chatter of the people around me gives me a sense of community."

This is the story of your life. Make it a happy, inspiring, colourful one.

Chapter 3 - Bring your "future you" into your present reality

Congratulations, you've made it to Chapter 3!

Either you've taken the time to write your story and you're pumped about the future you're about to create, or you're scanning through this book to see at which point exactly you'd like to request a refund. That's completely fine. Like I said in the introduction, the content of this book isn't for everyone. Irrespective of why you're here, I'm sure you're keen to see how you're going to create the reality of your dreams.

The four myths of being a successful entrepreneur

Let's first take a look at four of the most common beliefs around building a successful business which, until recently, I completely believed to be true.

1. You must work hard.
2. You must take massive action in order to succeed.
3. If you don't succeed, you've failed.
4. You must measure your success by your sales, profits, return on investment, etc.

Revisiting the four common beliefs of business success If you fully embrace the *Law of Attraction,* those tenets tend to lose their credibility. Let's take a closer look.

1. You must work hard

How many hard-working people do you know who are just about surviving? As an entrepreneur, I'm sure you've never worked as hard as you have been since starting your business. In the famous words of Dr Phil: How's that working for you? I thought so.

With the *Law of Attraction,* on the other hand, the only work you need to do is to pay attention to your thoughts and how they make you feel.

When you're feeling stressed, overwhelmed, doubtful, and worried - which is usually the mental state of the entrepreneur - your actions will feel like hard work. Because you're operating at a low vibration, you'll attract less than favourable results.

When you're taking action from a place of inspiration, you're operating at a higher vibration. Inspired action yields that "top of the world" feeling where it feels less like hard work and more like following your passion. When you're working from this higher vibration, you'll begin to notice how people and situations arise as and when you need them.

2. You must take massive action in order to succeed.

To me, there's nothing more damaging to an entrepreneur than being told to take massive action in order to succeed. It's that kind of advice that had me risk everything again and again in the past with disastrous results.

By all means, take massive action! But knowing what you now know about the *Law of Attraction*, please be careful not to confuse inspiration with desperation. Sometimes, all that's needed is a small change in perspective to achieve massive results. And that's what this book is all about.

3. If you haven't succeeded, you've failed.

Esther Hicks says it best. When you see a baby falling again and again when trying to walk, you don't say *"Get up, you little dummy!"* No! You clap your hands and cheer so that they know they're doing well and that it's all just part of their learning. Once they've mastered walking, you do the same to help them through their next benchmark.

So why should entrepreneurship be any different? When you think about it, you can't fail because life is an on-going, never-ending journey of highs and lows so you'll never really get it wrong because you'll never really get it done.

The absolute beauty of "failure" as we know it is that whenever it happens, an opposite desire is instantly created. Take a look at the story of your life as you want it to be. How much of your story stems from the failures or lacks in your past? If it weren't for all your perceived failures and disappointments, the story of your dream life wouldn't be nearly as exciting. So embrace the lows!

4. **You must measure your success by your sales, profits, return on investment, etc.**

As a Marketing Consultant, this one real hit home. If not by sales reports and Google Analytics, how was I supposed to measure the impact of a marketing campaign?

The flaw in my thinking was that I allowed external feedback—namely, those sales reports, Google analytic, and ROI— to determine my success so when sales were low, I'd be low. The key to the *Law of Attraction* is to pay more attention to your internal feedback, i.e. your feelings, because that, more than anything, determines whether your measurable results are going to be positive or negative.

Once I understood the impact of the *Law of Attraction* on the marketing results of a business, it became clear that my original book, "*The Ultimate Quickstart Guide to Marketing Strategy*", needed a total overhaul. Later in Part 2 of this book, I'll take you through my original thinking about marketing strategy and how it has changed since practicing the *Law of Attraction*.

The four steps of the Law of Attraction

How now, brown cow? If you take away the 4 most common business tenets, what's left?

Figure 6 - The end of marketing as I know it

The *Law of Attraction,* from the perspective of many teachers, comes down to four basic steps:

1. Ask. While you could actually just ask outright in thought or words, most of your asking has already been done through the contrasts you've experienced throughout your life. These contrasts make up the contents of the story of your life as you want it to be in Chapter 2.
2. Believe that everything you've asked for is created instantly on a vibrational level, ready for you to attract it.
3. Find a way to be in vibrational alignment so that you're able to attract what you've asked for.
4. From a place of vibrational alignment, be open for contrasts that will cause you to ask for even more.

An example of the *Law of Attraction* in action:

Say you've been struggling with the lack of money. That's step 1 done and dusted because all your wealth now lies in your vibrational reality. Step 2 is to believe that it's there, because when you believe it's there you stop trying to fix the problem of not having money. In other words, you change your thinking from one of poverty consciousness to one of prosperity consciousness. Step 3, because you're no longer focused on the lack of money, you're free to focus on better-feeling thoughts. By vibrating at this higher level, you automatically attract people and situations that will help you realise your desires.

Finally, in step 4, as life carries on from this place of high vibration, you welcome the contrasts that lower your vibration, knowing that they're simply indicators that you need to realign some areas of your life. If, for example, you become ill, a perfectly healthy version of yourself is automatically created in your vibrational reality. And the cycle continues...

Disclaimer: This is my interpretation of the four steps of the *Law of Attraction*. I've changed the wording, not the order, to better present the way in which I am able to implement it in my own life.

Ok, so this could very well be the point where you're reaching for the **Refund** button. I'm a practical person, and these steps seem rather "out there" for someone who's supposed to be taking their business seriously. But let's consider your choices. You could choose to carry on doing what you're doing with the same results, or you could give the *Law of Attraction* your best shot.

This chapter shares with you the trick that I use to make "airy-fairy" seem a tad more practical and easier to implement. I BRING THE "FUTURE ME" INTO MY PRESENT REALITY. What does this mean?

It means that not only do I write the story of my life the way I want it to be, I also describe the "future me" with the characteristics that would allow her to vibrate at the highest possible level in order to achieve her desires.

These characteristics include universal wisdom, unconditional love for myself and others, endless gratitude, self-acceptance, forgiveness, a kind heart, happiness, unyielding faith, the ability to see the good in everyone, and the understanding that people and situations who challenge me are there to expand my list of desires. And don't forget my business acumen and excellent decision-making skills!

What I'm actually doing is describing a version of myself that represents my higher consciousness. Depending on your spiritual beliefs, you could choose to see this as the version of yourself that's closest to God, closest to source, your soul, your essence, etc. Eckhart Tolle has an interesting take on this:

"*What a liberation to realise that the 'voice in my head' is not who I am. Who am I then? The one who sees it.*" If you choose not to bring spirituality into this, you could simply see it as the best version of yourself. For practical purposes, I prefer to view my higher consciousness as the best version of myself that knows how to put together the puzzle pieces as I go about collecting them on my life's journey.

Here are a few examples of how I bring the "future me" into my present reality. I may have said my way is practical...you be the judge. Remember, the ability to laugh at yourself contributes to a higher vibration so I do plenty of that!

1. I include at least one activity from the story of my life into my day-to-day activities. For example, I see the "future me" as being healthy and in shape, yet the present-day me hasn't been to pilates in 6 months! No more excuses. That was the inspiration I needed to get back to exercising.

2. We're humans. We get angry and we get annoyed. When I get the urge to throw things at people, I know that it's my present-day self vibrating at a lower level. Without judgement, I acknowledge the anger because it's trying to tell me something about myself, my personal boundaries and my expectations of other people. I take it as an indicator that some internal work needs to be done.

   Knowing that the "future me" understands that people and situations who challenge me are here to expand my list of desires, I thank them for my new desire. Perhaps it's people who don't annoy me. Perhaps it's more tolerance for people who don't share my views and I look for the good in them... often from a safe distance until I'm ready to deal with them face to face.

3. When I get overwhelmed with a situation, I actually speak to my "future me". I'd say something along the lines of *"Ok, you sort this one out, I'm going to binge watch a series."* The fact is that doing something fun will raise my vibration and bring clarity to the situation anyway. The feeling that you can surrender your troubles to someone else just adds an extra sense of peace. This is very powerful when you integrate your spiritual beliefs into your business.

Now for the most important part of this book: Whenever you're engaged in an activity that brings your future you into your present reality, it is important that you repeat these words: *"I am so grateful to be living the life of my dreams. I love my life!"*

When it comes to the *Law of Attraction,* the only moment that counts is the present moment so even if you're feeling like you're living the life of your dreams just for that moment, the *Law of Attraction* has to respond. The great thing about the *Law of Attraction* is that you don't have to be vibrating at the highest level all the time to start seeing results. You just need to be vibrating at a higher level more than you do at a lower level and then watch as the miracles show up. Are you still with me? Great! It's exercise time.

Exercise 2

Here's a short exercise before we get into the business of running a business in Part 2.

- Describe the characteristics inherent in your "future you".

- From your story in Exercise 1, choose the activities that you'll be incorporating into your day-to-day activities. Commit to it. This forms your action plan for manifesting your dream life.

The more opportunities you create to tell yourself that you're "...so grateful to be living the life of my dreams" the sooner you'll start to see miracles unfold in your life.

PART 2: Let's get down to business

Chapter 4 - Get clear on the definition of marketing

If there could be only one gem you've taken from Part 1, I sincerely hope it's the knowledge that you can create any life you desire simply by focusing on how you think. You've been doing it all your life! If your current reality isn't exactly what you would've liked it to be, it's only because you've been spending more time thinking more about the negative than you have about the positive.

While it's hard to swallow, it should also be empowering to know that you can change it in an instant by changing the way you think.

One BIG caveat before we carry on… What you think and what you feel need to be in alignment because the *Law of Attraction* responds to what you feel, not what you think. Try it. Say something like *"I'm going to make $1 million in the next two weeks."*

Does saying that get you all pumped about being a millionaire in the next two weeks? I didn't think so. That's because you don't really believe that you'll be making $1 million in the next two weeks. Because you don't believe what you're thinking, your underlying feeling is one of doubt, disbelief, and a whole bunch of negative emotions that are leading you down a path you're actually trying to avoid. So stop that thought right there!

For most of us, our business is the vehicle for building the life of our dreams. While I'm all for lofty goals and big dreams, it's often those big dreams that trip us up because we really don't believe we have what it takes to achieve them. And then we wonder why we don't!

Another caveat: While I believe with all my heart that cultivating a healthy mindset is the first step to a successful business, this book isn't about making you a better person. If I were to do that, I'd be implying that you're not good enough exactly as you are. We're all perfect exactly as we are.

This book simply challenges you to change the way you think. It gives you an alternative to believing you need to fix yourself, your business, or your situation in order to succeed. Your only "hard work" is to master your thoughts. When you do that, the right people, the right teachers and the right situations will make their way to you as and when you need them to.

In Part 1, I shared with you some of my tricks for living the life of my dreams from one moment to the next. In Part 2, I'll show you how to use those tricks for running the business of your dreams from one moment to the next.

Now let's talk marketing…

Based on a text-book definition, marketing can be defined as a *"PROCESS of bringing PEOPLE to a PLACE where they PERFORM AN ACTION that leads to the selling of a PRODUCT/SERVICE at a PROFIT."* Figure 7 illustrates how this definition of marketing applies.

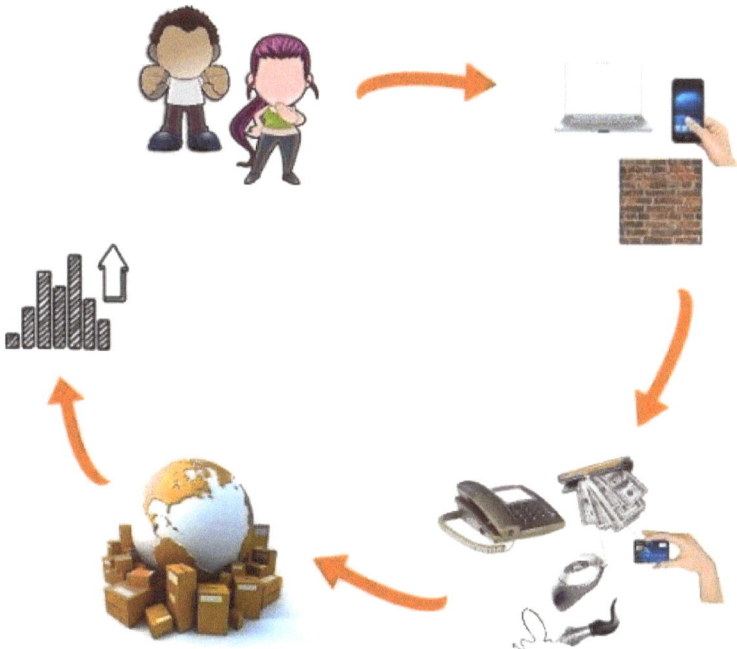

Figure 7 - The definition of marketing

In Part 2, I'll show you how to use the *Law of Attraction* to tackle this process with clarity and focus.

Chapter 5 - Choose your business model

So...who am I talking to here?

Either you're a new or soon-to-be business owner ready to take on the world, or you're a seasoned entrepreneur who's ready and willing to make a serious shift in your thinking. For the purpose of this exercise, I'm going to be speaking to the oldies. If you're a newbie, it's still worth a read as it will help you to focus your new business.

A reminder: The purpose of a business is to make money by selling goods and services at a profit. In order to determine what to sell and how to profit from it, you need to choose a business model, which is a high-level plan for how your business is going to make money.

Basically, a business model can fall in two broad categories:

1. Selling your own products
2. Selling someone else's products

Selling your own products include services, memberships, digital products and physical products. It entails manufacturing it, packaging it, selling it and delivering it. When you're selling someone else's products, you're either an affiliate where they're responsible for delivering the product to the buyer and you receive a commission or a referral fee; or you're a reseller where you sell the product for a mark-up and you're responsible for delivering it to the buyer.

- Product owner
- Affiliate
- Reseller

Usually when we choose our business model, we look at which option will make the most money the fastest. Based on basic business principles, that seems like the right thing to do. But not according to the *Law of Attraction.*

When it comes to marketing the *Law of Attraction* way, any decision based purely on the making of money is rooted in the lack of money. It implies that you need to place effort into making something happen when it should be about effortless creation and allowing what's already in your future to flow into your present.

So instead, ask yourself what your business model would look like if success was guaranteed. If your future was allowed to flow into your life, what would it look like?

For myself, I've combined my love for entrepreneurs, marketing, and writing into a service in which I create content for small businesses, including strategy development, marketing content, e-books, courses, and reports. I have recently included workshops and meetups as I did in the past because, as useful as the Internet is, it doesn't replace the intimacy of face-to-face interactions.

When choosing your business model, think about what you enjoy doing, what you're good at, and how you prefer to spend your time. Take a look at the stories you wrote in Chapters 2 and 3 for some clues.

For example, here's mine: "*I have learnt that sharing my failures and successes through writing has helped others who are experiencing the same to cope a little easier. And I don't always have to have a solution! This helps me create meaningful blog posts, e-books, and courses that resonate with the right people. I also know that working just for the money brings my vibration to an all-time low so my business requires that I work with clients who contribute to society in meaningful ways. And although I enjoy the tiny details of everything, I'm in my element when I'm conceptualising and putting together the bigger picture. That's why strategy development excites me. By being a writer, marketer, and facilitator, I've developed a business that allows me to be creative, selective, intimate, and maybe make a difference in people's lives. Perfect!*"

Now that you've pinned down your future business model, it's time to put on your thinking hats. Being an entrepreneur requires you to wear many hats in one day. The biggest mistake we make is to try to wear all these hats ourselves, often at the same time. Imagine the chaos in a day if we were to literally switch hats each time we needed to perform a task or make a decision!

Figure 8 - The different hats of a business owner

So take a few moments to think this through. What is your ideal day as a business owner? What are your strengths? What do you thrive on? What would you rather not do yourself? Do you prefer working in a team? Do you enjoy managing people? Are you a great networker or motivator?

Here's an exercise to help you tell the story of your business the way you want it to be. Make a list of the 10 must-have requirements of your dream business and call it List A. My List A looks something like this:

1. Enables me to work with people from anywhere in the world

2. Enables me to choose my own hours
3. Generates income from various sources
4. Requires very little admin from my side
5. Allows me to work with clients who inspire me
6. Allows me to work on projects that allow me to learn and grow
7. Has the ability to run successfully without me
8. Has the support of knowledgeable, honest, trustworthy team
9. Gives me enough time to do what I love with the people that I love
10. Gives me the financial freedom to do what I want with the people that I love

Now on a different page, compile List B. For List B, write down everything from your past and present businesses that caused you anger, discomfort, annoyance, or frustration.

You have your List B? Now for the fun part. Knowing that everything in your past that angered, annoyed, or frustrated you was just there to launch an equal and opposite rocket of desire, turn every item on List B into its equal and opposite must-have on List A. Say my List B included unreliable business partners and business processes that caused major bottlenecks, my continued List A would look like this:

11. Reliable and accountable business partners
12. Efficient business processes

Next is to turn my list into the way I want it to be.

Exercise 3

Let's seal the deal by turning your list into a story about your business the way you want it to be. Remember to use words such as *"love"*, *"appreciate"*, *"grateful"* so that it becomes a powerful story filled with positive affirmations.

Here's mine: "*I love that my business enables me to work with people anywhere in the world and choose my own hours. I am grateful that it generates income from various sources with very little admin from my side. I am truly thankful for clients who inspire me and projects that allow me to learn and grow. I particularly appreciate that my business can run successfully without me because I have the support of a knowledgeable, honest, trustworthy team; reliable and accountable business partners; and efficient business processes. This gives me enough time and financial freedom to do what I love with the people that I love, for which I am eternally grateful.*"

Chapter 6 - Identify your customer

Suppose John, Kelly, Mike, Cindy, and Travis in Figure 9 are all potential buyers of your product.

Figure 9 - Potential buyers. Or not!

- John's a professional and a bit of a know-it-all. He's always online, mostly on forums speaking his mind, and he's subscribed to various business newsletters and blogs because he prefers news being delivered to him. Living by a schedule, he begins each morning reading the newspaper while having his coffee. Your challenge would be convincing him that your product is the best solution for his problem.

- Kelly's a flirt and used to people pandering around her whims. Her fabulous life's always on display on social media as she soaks up the attention. Your challenge would be to keep your cool while catering to her unrealistic demands.

- Mike's laid back. An online gamer, he tries to do as much as possible without leaving the comfort of his home. If you suggested he tried your product, he probably would. Your challenge would be getting his attention long enough for him to hear your message!

- Nobody messes with Cindy! If she finds a fault in your product or service, she'll be all over Facebook before you can say "*Let's sort it o...*" When she's not complaining about bad service or life in general, she's probably at the mall spreading her sunshine. Your challenge would be to keep her happy at every stage of her buying decision.

- Poor Travis...He's the frazzled father of young twins so whatever you're selling, there needs to be doubles (especially if it's a little something to calm his nerves). Your challenge would be to fight off all the other information buzzing around in his mind and convince him that what you're selling can simplify his life.

Would you like to have any of these people as potential buyers? Probably not.

In the past, this is where I would adamantly argue that understanding your target market was the first step to a successful marketing strategy. If you don't understand them, how would you know how to market to them? I would then recommend some research into popular keywords and niches that make money that would help you build the profile of the perfect customer.

Since incorporating the *Law of Attraction* into my own business, that doesn't seem to make much sense anymore... If you don't get your own house in order, you'll end up attracting the wrong people no matter how spot-on your targeting is. So best you up that vibration first!

Something to think about: If you were choosing your target market based on the people you'd most like to serve instead of the people most likely to buy your products and services, how would you describe them? How would you add value to their lives? How would you get rewarded financially and otherwise? Compile List A of the characteristics inherent in the people you'd like to serve. Take a look at my list to get you started.

List A:

1. Desire for personal growth
2. Willingness to embrace change
3. Have a prosperity mindset
4. Driven by passion and purpose
5. Entrepreneurial and innovative
6. Willing to invest in themselves and their business
7. Kind and generous
8. Fun-loving and good natured
9. Open-minded and non-judgemental
10. Offer a heart-based service instead of a purely profit-driven service

Now do the same as in Chapter 4. Compile List B of your past annoyances, then rewrite them as the equal and opposite desire and add to List A. My expanded List A now looks like this.

From clients who didn't pay me on time or value my services, and operated from a place of disorganisation and chaos, my ideal clients:

11. Pay me on time
12. See the value in what I do
13. Have structured processes
14. Are committed to the success of their own businesses

Exercise 4

You know the drill for the next step. Rewrite your list as the story of your customers the way you want it to be using words such as *"love"*, *"appreciate"*, *"grateful"*. Let it be a powerful story filled with all the wonderful characteristics your customers will exude.

Here's mine... *"I absolutely love that my clients desire personal growth as much as they desire business growth, and I appreciate their willingness to embrace change. I am truly thankful that their prosperity mindset, passion, and purpose make it a pleasure for me to serve them. Their entrepreneurial and innovative spirit allows me to learn from them, for which I am grateful. Because of their fun-loving and good-natured personalities, projects are fun!*

It is a safe, open-minded and non-judgmental space where all perspectives are respected and appreciated. I am grateful that my clients offer a heart-based service instead of a purely profit-driven service. I love their willingness to invest in themselves and their business while being kind and generous towards others.

I am truly grateful that they are well structured, organised, see the value in what I do and pay me on time. Together, we are committed to the success of their business and the people they serve."

Chapter 7 - Design your marketing message

If you've been watching the Internet marketing scene for even a little while, you may have noticed some tacky sales pitches doing their rounds.

As an old-school marketer, it leaves a bitter taste in my mouth as I find that purely sales-driven marketing is closer to manipulation than marketing. While there may be immediate rewards to this sales-driven type of marketing, it usually entails a large amount of effort to sustain the income.

On the other hand, the *Law of Attraction* has authenticity at its core and even though the financial rewards may not be immediately visible, it gives you a recipe for effortless living.

The *Law of Attraction* turns traditional marketing messaging on its head: It's not about telling potential buyers what they need to hear in order for you to sell them a product. It's about expressing yourself and attracting those who are ready to hear it. In other words, it's got everything to do with your own authentic expression and nothing to do with your potential readers. How's that for a shift in thinking?

"*But what does this mean?*" I hear you ask.

It comes down to one question, methinks. If you take the exchange of money out of the equation, why are you selling what you're selling? If you believe in what you're selling and you reconnect with why you're selling it, you should be able to speak about it from a place of authenticity. What you say will resonate with some and not with others, and that's ok! You only want to work with those vibrating on your level anyway so you better make sure it's a good one.

Here's my message to you, for example.

TITLE: Are you tired of being stressed, cash-strapped, and tired?

According to the Law of Attraction, making money shouldn't be so hard! Maybe it's time you just allowed the shift to hit the fan. I said "shift"...

In this book, I urge you to make a shift in your thinking and give up the control you think you have to fix your business. You may feel like chaos is about to erupt because you're not there putting out the fires. But if you focus simply on "being" instead of "doing", you'll begin to notice that life has a way of sorting itself out.

Aim to find a silver lining to every cloud from one moment to the next. Breathe in calm. Be excited about what's to come. Once you've mastered "being", you'll start to notice a clear path for what you should be "doing". The Law of Attraction never fails.

You're reading my book and you're hearing my message. Either it resonates with you and you'll hang around and do the exercises, or it doesn't resonate with you and you won't even finish the book. Should I be concerned about those who don't find value in what I'm saying? Well, not really. How other people behave shouldn't really be any of my business, according to the *Law of Attraction.* My only business is to focus on how I'm feeling and ensure that, while I write, my message is from the heart and with the intention of bringing about positive change in the lives of some of the readers.

That's also how it works in your personal life. If you start living in a way that raises your vibration, you may notice old friends fading out of your life and new friends appearing.

Exercise 5

So what is your heartfelt message about the product that you're selling? If you could tell a story about why you're offering it to them, what would that story be? Give it a title and a body of around 10 lines as I did in my example.

Chapter 8 - Bring your vibration into your marketing

In previous versions, this chapter began with: *"This wouldn't be a book about marketing if we didn't talk about money. The harsh reality is that it costs money to market your business. Don't let anybody tell you otherwise!"*

In this version, I'm taking money completely out of it. While it's true that marketing your business may cost money, the focus of this chapter isn't on how to spend your money. This chapter focuses on how to best spend your energy so that you can allow money to flow naturally.

HEREIN LIES THE CRUX OF IT: YOU MANAGE YOUR ENERGY BY MANAGING YOUR EMOTIONS.

ARE YOU MAKING MARKETING DECISIONS FROM A SPACE OF FEAR, DOUBT, DISEMPOWERMENT, CONFUSION, OR ANY OF THE NEGATIVE EMOTIONS THAT KEEP YOU FEELING FRUSTRATED? DO YOU FEEL LIKE YOU'RE CONSTANTLY CHASING MONEY, CLIENTS, OR RESULTS?

When you're aiming **to attract money,** you should really not be thinking of money at all, especially when thoughts of money bring you down! Think about what you're feeling in the moment and **always choose a thought that feels better.** In other words, raise your vibration.

And **when you're spending money**, know that **inspired spending will actually attract more money.** When you're spending your money—be it paying your bills or spoiling yourself—make sure you find a way to feel good about the money going out. If you don't, it means you're operating with a poverty consciousness and you'll get that thrown right back at you.

If you embrace your spending with the certainty that any gaps will be filled, you'll get that thrown right back at you. Which would you rather have? Note: Inspired spending doesn't mean reckless spending, though! Don't try to fool the *Law of Attraction*. First get into vibrational alignment and then spend.

That's the basis of *vibrational marketing.*

When it comes to **traditional marketing**, it's about making decisions with your head, which often leads to chaos. You need to constantly keep abreast of the current marketing tools, customer trends, and technological advancement in order to make feasible marketing decisions. You're driven by the next customer, the next sale, and profits. With life being as busy as it is, who has time for that?

With **vibrational marketing,** you learn to listen to your heart's intelligence. You make marketing decisions from a place of peace.

So this is roundabouts where I lose most readers so this time around, I'm bringing in pictures to demonstrate head-centred thinking versus heart-centred thinking.

Thinking with your head versus thinking with your heart

In Figure 10, the "before" drawing is me thinking with my head and the "after" is me thinking with my heart.

Before

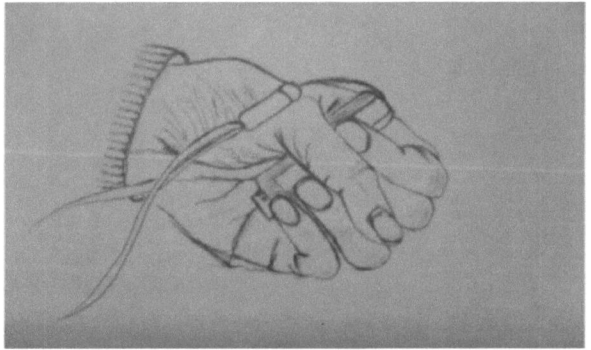

After

Figure 10 - Finding my inner genius in 20 minutes

As part of a task for a 3-day Creategy (Creative Strategy) course run by University of Cape Town back in the day, the "before" picture, which I picked up on Google, accurately sums up my attempt on that day when the lecturer said: *"Draw your hand."*

Clearly, I'm no Picasso.

The "after" picture happened when I switched off my brain. In the exercise, we were taught to switch off the logical, judgemental, *"you can't do this"* part of our brains and trust our natural ability to create something beyond what we thought was possible for ourselves. Suddenly, I was an artist! Without thinking, some other mechanism kicked in as I got into the flow of creating something I didn't think was possible in me.

As a side note, anybody can do this and here's the trick...

Choose any object you'd like to draw. For 20 minutes, draw it while LOOKING AWAY from the paper you're drawing on. Yes, you'll be drawing scribbles, but your mind doesn't know that. It's paying attention to the details of said object and not caring about what you're doing on the paper. The self-criticism is switched off and you get so caught up in the details of your hand that you forget everything else. You get into flow.

After twenty minutes, draw it again, this time looking at the paper when you're drawing. You'll notice that your mind automatically remembers the details and you're creating from an entirely different space.

IMPORTANT POINT #1: The moral of the story is that we're all intuitively creative in the right environment without the negative emotions and self-limiting beliefs holding us back. We're able to create from a place of inner peace.

Figure 11 shows the "before" and "after" pictures of me solving a problem with my head versus solving a problem with my heart using a biofeedback system that measures my heart-mind coherence.

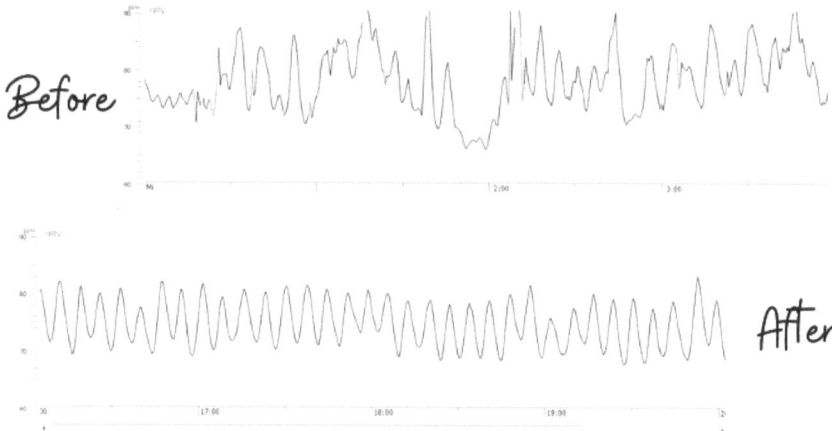

Figure 11 - Thinking with my head versus thinking with my heart

What is heart-mind coherence? If you're as old as I am, you were brought up to believe that the brain was the thinker and told the body what to do. Recent science has discovered that the heart has a little brain, too. There is constant communication between the heart and the brain, and the heart can actually tell the brain which chemicals to release into the body.

The "before" picture was captured when my heart and my brain were not talking the same language. I was in fight-or-flight mode, thinking with my brain and not listening to my heart. The "after" picture is me slowing down my breathing, finding a place of neutrality and calm, and choosing a better-feeling thought so that my heart and mind were in coherence. From that space of peace, I was able to see the possibilities instead of the problems.

IMPORTANT POINT #2: Remember chapter 1? Heart-mind coherence plays a vital role in your level of vibration and the people you naturally attract into your life. It's no longer just about having the right mindset. It's about having the right heart-mind-set.

What's this got to do with marketing?

In chapter 4, I suggested a text-book definition of marketing can be defined as a *"PROCESS of bringing PEOPLE to a PLACE where they PERFORM AN ACTION that leads to the selling of a PRODUCT/SERVICE at a PROFIT."*

I'd now like to challenge **OUR** thinking. If vibrational marketing has nothing to do with money and everything to do with vibration, what if marketing for the new world is a *"PROCESS of bringing PEOPLE to a PLACE where they PERFORM AN ACTION that leads to **PEACE**"*?

What if business in the new world isn't about being profit-driven, but peace-driven? Imagine the impact you could bring to the world if that joy you feel when doing what you love can be shared with the world to create joy, which then automatically generates profit?

Bear with me. In the next chapter, we'll put it all together into a Vibrational Marketing Strategy that is driven by joy.

Exercise 6

First let's raise your vibration by recapping all your exercises and get you out of mind-centred thinking back to heart-centred thinking. Got your notes? Read them aloud a few times until you feel warm and fuzzy. If it doesn't make you feel warm and fuzzy, it's a sign that you may need to retweak them.

Exercise 1:

Try writing the story of your life the way you want it to be. Include all the activities you love and those you'd like to participate in if time and money were no longer an issue.

Exercise 2:

- Describe the characteristics inherent in your "future you".
- From your story in exercise 1, choose the activities that you'll be incorporating into your day-to-day activities. Commit to it. This forms your action plan for manifesting your dream life.

The more opportunities you create to tell yourself that you're "...so grateful to be living the life of my dreams" the sooner you'll start to see miracles unfold in your life.

Exercise 3:

Let's seal the deal by turning your list into a story about your business the way you want it to be. Remember to use words such as "love", "appreciate", "grateful" so that it becomes a powerful story filled with positive affirmations.

Exercise 4:

You know the drill for the next step... Rewrite your list as the story of your customers the way you want it to be using words such as "love", "appreciate", "grateful". Let it be a powerful story filled with all the wonderful characteristics your customers will exude.

Exercise 5:

So what is your heartfelt message about the product that you're selling? If you could tell a story about why you're offering it to them, what would that story be? Give it a title and a body of around 10 lines as I did in my example.

Chapter 9 - Putting it into practice

Whether traditional marketing or vibrational marketing, it's always going to be about getting new clients. It's simply the energy behind marketing that we're aiming to change. Instead of measuring the success of your marketing activities by the profits, you measure it by whether or not you're feeling peace.

So back to some marketing basics. Potential clients, customers, or partners go through four decision-making stages before deciding that you're it:

1. They become aware.
2. They search for more information.
3. They're ready to make the purchase.
4. They've made the purchase and they're either happy, unhappy, or disinterested because they're already moved on to the next product.

As a marketer, your role is to meet them at each of these stages:

1. Create awareness.
2. Provide an engaging space for them to obtain the information they need quickly and easily.
3. Facilitate the commitment.
4. Inspire involvement.

At which frequency are you vibrating when you make the connection? When you see customers as money in the bank, they'll instinctively pick up on it.

Consider how many Facebook ads, YouTube ads, and promotional emails you ignore. Also consider how many Facebook ads, YouTube ads, and promotional emails you love reading. Even if the content is the same as the ones you ignore, it's the energy behind the content that either resonates with you or it doesn't.

In the same way, your audience will pick up on your intention. Whether you're creating on your own or within a group; whether you're sharing with one person or to a group, you need to embody Spirit when you step into whatever marketing hat you're wearing.

Time for a short exercise. Take a few deep breaths in and out, bringing your attention to your heart.

1. Remember a time you were creating something alone... a product, an article, a book, graphics, marketing content, artwork... whatever makes you happy. When you're **creating by yourself from a higher vibration,** you're deepening your connection between yourself and the energy that created you (whomever or whatever you believe that to be) so affirm: *"Knowing myself as an embodiment of Spirit, I am creativity."*

   Repeat it a couple of times so that you feel the emotion. You may notice that it inspires more creativity.

2. Now remember creating within a group. It could be a collaboration, a partnership, a community, or an informal chat. When you're **creating within a group from a higher vibration,** you're expanding your consciousness by tapping into your inherent ability to connect deeply with others so affirm: *"Knowing myself as an embodiment of Spirit, I am empathy."*

   Repeat it a couple of times so that you feel the emotion of connecting with others from a place of empathy. You may notice that it inspires more empathy.

3. Suppose your product is complete and you're ready to share it with the world. When you're vibrating at a high frequency and you're **sharing your joy with one person,** you're using heart-mind coherence to connect heart-to-heart and intuitively know how to respond to their needs. Remember a time when you were telling someone about your offering and the words just naturally flowed as you answered all their questions. Now affirm: *"Knowing myself as an embodiment of Spirit, I am omniscience."*

   Repeat it a couple of times so that you feel the emotion of being all-knowing. You may notice that it inspires further insights.

4. When you're vibrating at a high frequency and you're **sharing your joy with groups of people,** you intuitively know that there is enough of everything for everyone. Remember a time when you were telling a group of people about your offering, and you were overflowing with gratitude for their presence and support. Affirm: *"Knowing myself as an embodiment of Spirit, I am abundance."*

   Repeat it a couple of times so that you feel abundant. You may notice that it inspires further feelings of abundance.

Figure 12 illustrates how these vibrational marketing affirmations fit together.

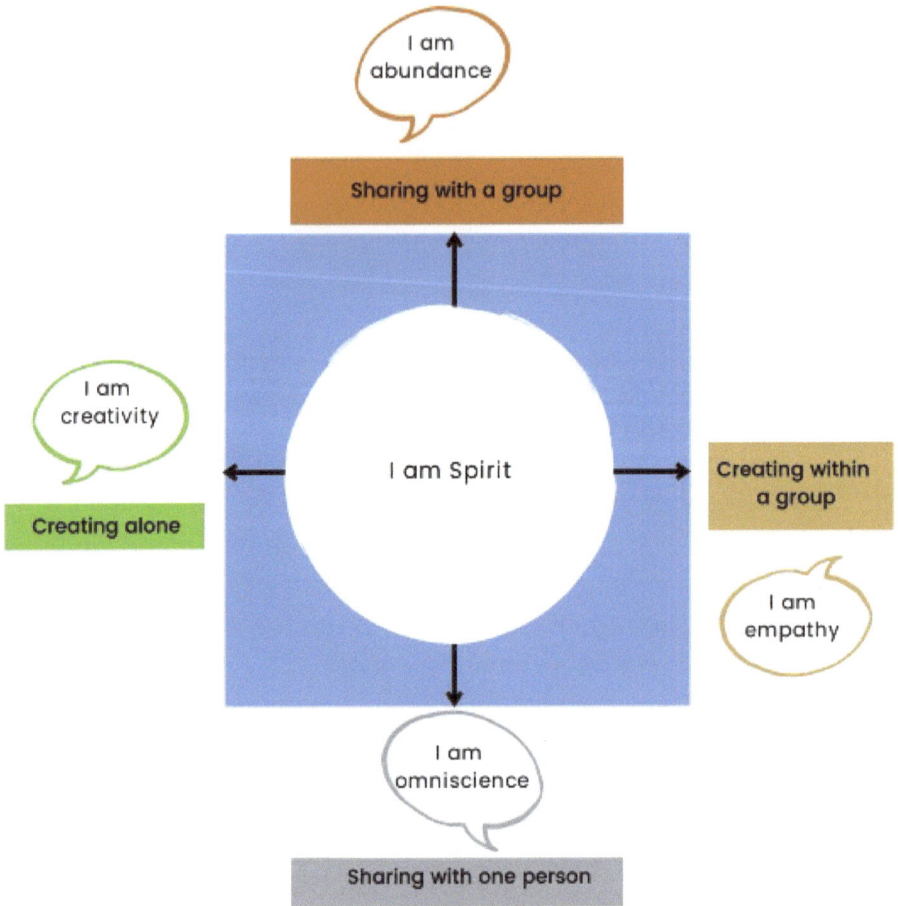

Figure 12 - Affirmations for Vibrational Marketing

The key to making vibrational marketing work for you is to truly embody these elements. Figure 13 illustrates what happens to your vibration when you consistently and mindfully choose thoughts that make you feel better, and when you make marketing decisions from the heart and not with your mind.

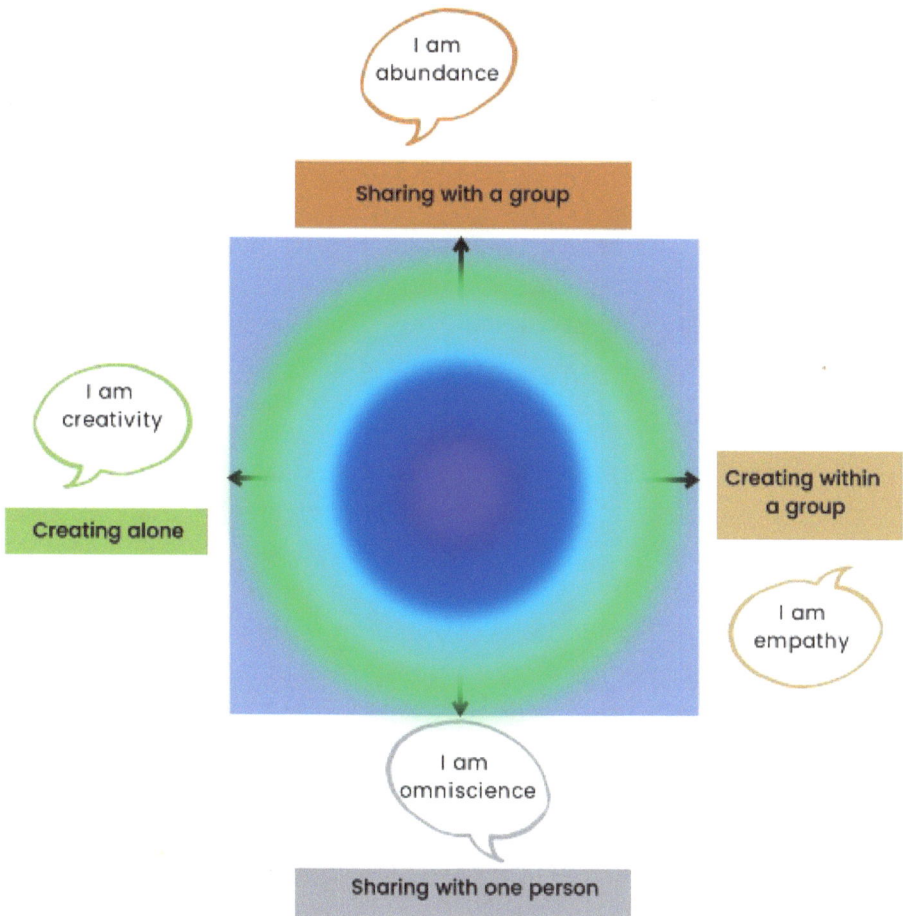

Figure 13 - The effects of living "as Spirit" on your vibration

By mindfully choosing to make marketing decisions from a higher vibration knowing yourself as Spirit, low-vibrating emotions, such as fear, guilt, shame, depression, and disempowerment no longer have a place in your life.

And as you move through life with this mindfulness, you have no choice but to attract the ideal clients, the perfect partners, the unimaginable opportunities, and the flow of abundance. That's the essence of using the *Law of Attraction* as your marketing strategy!

Consider your marketing challenges as already solved and revel in the moment. Seeing your problem as already solved invokes the *Law of Attraction* and you automatically attract solutions. Your only job from there on out is to listen to your heart's guidance as you make marketing decisions that align with who you are at your core.

With **vibrational marketing,** the focus is on ensuring that you are vibrating at your highest possible frequency at each stage of your customer's journey. According to the *Law of Attraction,* they will automatically respond to you.

1. **When creating alone...** How are you authentically expressing your **inherent creativity?** What is the unique marketing message from your heart to theirs? Which platforms are you using to convey this message?
2. **When providing an engaging space for those wanting to know more...** How are you using **empathy** to tap into what your community members, colleagues, or partners need? In which ways are you using your six senses instead of hearing only with your ears and seeing only with your eyes?
3. **When facilitating the commitment...** Knowing that you are **omniscient** and can access all the details you need simply by raising your vibration, how can you connect heart-to-heart in a way that's unique to their needs?
4. **When inspiring involvement...** Knowing that there's an **abundance** of everything for everyone, how can you continue to add value to your clients? How can you get them involved in making this world a better place for everyone?

As an entrepreneur, you have tremendous power. Imagine a marketing strategy where the end goal is to resonate peace so that those receiving your marketing message can receive peace. Where you resonate creativity, empathy, omniscience, abundance, and unconditional love so those you connect with receive creativity, empathy, omniscience, abundance, and unconditional love.

You won't need to know the details. You won't need to have all the answers. Just be yourself as the Spirit energy you are and let the answers find you. Manifestation will follow… it's the law.

So knowing what you now know about frequency, vibration, and resonance, my wish is that you use this power to help heal the world no matter what product or service you offer...you simply need to BE love when you share it with the world.

And don't forget the steps for making the *Law of Attraction* your marketing strategy:

1. Ask. Manifestation will follow because it's the *Law of Attraction,* so give yourself permission to dream big!
2. Believe that everything you've asked for is created instantly on a vibrational level, ready for you to attract it.
3. Find a way to be in vibrational alignment so that you're able to allow what you've asked for - or something even better - to manifest.
4. From a place of vibrational alignment, be open for contrasts that will cause you to ask for even more.

Exercise 7

Knowing myself as Spirit, I am able to create a story around my marketing strategy that keeps me inspired…

I am so grateful that I can focus my **creativity** *on writing articles, ebooks, and courses on topics that inspire me.*

I am in awe that my work inspires millions of readers all over the world as I tap into my **omniscience** *and connect their dots through my writing.*

*I love building my community as I am able to empathise with the people I connect with using my **empathy.***

*As **abundance,** I am so appreciative of my marketing partners who consistently bring in new customers. I am grateful for my service providers who are doing an amazing job promoting my books and giving me magnificent returns on my marketing investments.*

And I am absolutely grateful that I can pursue my passions and my purpose in all that I do knowing my dreams are naturally turning into reality.

Most importantly, I am at peace knowing that it's on its way and my job is to take one inspired step at a time towards inspiring everyone I connect with.

As I have, rewrite your marketing strategy with gratitude for being able to focus on doing what you love doing and the impact you'll inevitably make. For now, you don't have to know the details as each inspired step will be revealed at the right time.

Additional tips, tools, and tricks

You deserve a medal for making it this far! Please connect with me if you need any further assistance in developing your vibrational marketing strategy. Here are a few additional tips.

The underlying premise of the *Law of Attraction* is to raise your vibration in any situation. While it's a simple rule, it certainly isn't easy! So here are a few tips for getting you through those negative vibes.

1. Make peace with where you are wherever you are. Don't get angry or frustrated when you're feeling angry and frustrated. Acknowledge it without dwelling too long then add its opposite equal to your growing list of desires.

2. Don't judge your progress by your current reality. Things take time and when your focus is on what's NOT manifesting, it's always going to NOT manifest. Rather, judge your progress on how you feel. If you've found a way to make peace with where you are, you're on the right path to manifesting.

3. Always choose a better-feeling thought. For example, what feels better? *"This job sucks!"* OR *"I'm really happy that this job is only temporary. My dream job is in my vibrational reality so it must be in the making"*?

4. Distinguish between your need for something and your desire for something. Need is focusing on the lack of it while desire is focusing on what's in your vibrational reality with certainty that it's on its way. See what feels better: *"I need a car to get around"* vs. *"My [insert dream car here] will be parked in my driveway really soon!"*

5. Distract yourself! When you distract yourself, you stop the momentum of the negative thought. For example, challenge yourself to find 10 fruits or veg that begin with the letter "A", or go through the alphabet naming songs that begin with that letter. Be silly, have fun, don't Google!

6. Sing, dance, draw, write, paint…you don't have to be good at it, you just have to enjoy it.

Final words

As I'm ready to release this book into the world for the final time, I look back at the five years of tweaking, shelving, revising, and rewriting and I realise it reflects my own personal growth. Most importantly, it reflects my struggle with self-love, self-acceptance, and a lifetime of self-limiting beliefs.

Over these past five years, my peace has been fleeting. Knowing all the rules of being easy-going is much simpler than implementing them!

Referring back to the scale of consciousness from chapter one, it was only when I began peeling through the negative layers of shame, guilt, worry, grief, blame, and fear that I started to desire something more for myself. Only when I deepened by connection to Spirit by choosing to think with my heart and not my head—when I began to make creativity, omniscience, empathy, and abundance my natural state—did I begin to fully claim my space in this world.

Figure 14 probably best illustrates the challenge with my thoughts and emotions over time.

Figure 14 - My vibrational growth over time

Now, my life is fast filling up with love, joy, and peace as I willingly accept who I am, flaws and all. I still have those negative emotions, but they're simply reminders that I am human after all. I now live with each day in complete faith that everything I desire is on its way. That's how the *Law of Attraction* works without fail.

If anything, this book is my invitation to you to live in faith: What we do for ourselves, we do for others and now, more than ever, the world needs faith.

Happy manifesting!

Next steps

1. For more about my *Vibrational Marketing Mentoring,* please visit my website: [Vibrational Marketing Mentor](#)

2. And if you'd like to learn more about how I can help you put together a *Vibrational Marketing Strategy* for energetically impacting the world, let's chat.

allisonwentworthross.com

calendly.com/colossally/one-on-one

allison@simplycolossal.com